T0193440

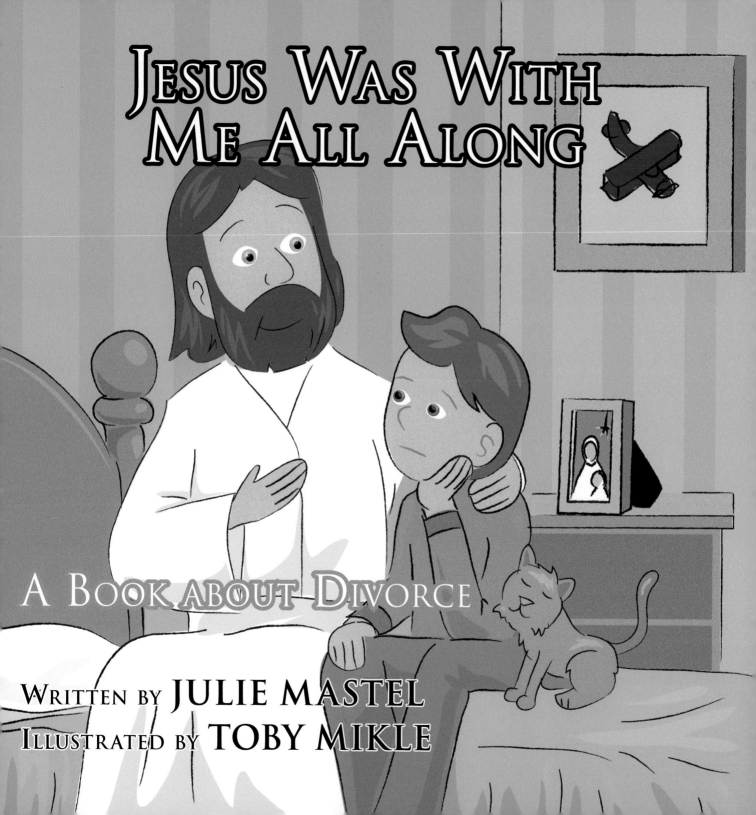

Jesus Was With Me All Along

A Book about Divorce

Written by JULIE MASTEL

Illustrated by TOBY MIKLE

WestBow Press books may be ordered through booksellers or by contacting:

WestBow Press
A Division of Thomas Nelson & Zondervan
1663 Liberty Drive
Bloomington, IN 47403
www.westbowpress.com
844-714-3454

Because of the dynamic nature of the Internet, any web addresses or links contained in this book may have changed since publication and may no longer be valid. The views expressed in this work are solely those of the author and do not necessarily reflect the views of the publisher, and the publisher hereby disclaims any responsibility for them.

Certain stock imagery © Thinkstock.

Scriptures taken from the Holy Bible, New International Version®, NIV®. Copyright © 1973, 1978, 1984, 2011 by Biblica, Inc.™ Used by permission of Zondervan. All rights reserved worldwide. www.zondervan.com The "NIV" and "New International Version" are trademarks registered in the United States Patent and Trademark Office by Biblica, Inc.™ All rights reserved.

ISBN: 978-1-4908-0162-9 (sc)
ISBN: 978-1-4908-0163-6 (e)

Library of Congress Control Number: 2013912411

Print information available on the last page.

WestBow Press rev. date: 02/24/2021

WESTBOW
PRESS®
A DIVISION OF THOMAS NELSON
& ZONDERVAN

When I was younger my
parents got divorced...

...but Jesus was with
me all along.

2

I thought it was my fault and I felt sad.

3

But then I realized it wasn't because of me.

My parents just couldn't work things out.

But Jesus was with me all along.

They would fight sometimes
and that scared me.

7

Then one day my mom went to live somewhere else, and I didn't understand why.

8

I stayed at home with my dad.

Later I lived with my mom at her new place.

There were times
when I felt alone...

...but Jesus was with me all along.

Later my dad and mom both got married again, so I had two sets of parents instead of one.

I found out there were other kids just like me.

14

The other kids knew how I felt, but
more importantly Jesus knew.

Remember that He sees your pain and He loves you. He has been with you all along.

16

The LORD himself goes before you and will be with you; He will never leave you nor forsake you. Do not be afraid; do not be discouraged." Deut. 31:8

Printed in the United States
By Bookmasters